WITH A CAMERA IN THE GHETTO

WITH A CAMERA IN THE GHETTO

MENDEL GROSSMAN

Edited by Zvi Szner and Alexander Sened

With text from *The Chronicle of the Lodz Ghetto,*
edited by Lucjan Dobroszycki and Danuta Dombrowska

SCHOCKEN BOOKS · NEW YORK

Most of the photographs contained in this album were copied not from the negatives, which were lost, but from prints found in various places after the war. The following have done a great deal to make this possible: the late photographer's sister, Shoshana Grossman-Zylbersztajn, many of his friends, and especially Nahman Sonnabend and Arieh Ben-Menahem. We are also indebted to the memorial authority Yad Vashem which placed at our disposal the photographs in its archives.

The texts accompanying the photographs were taken from the two volumes of *The Chronicle of the Lodz Ghetto,* which appeared in Polish, in Lodz, in 1965 and 1967, edited by Lucjan Dobroszycki and Danuta Dombrowska.

English: Mendel Kohansky

Layout by Peter Merom

First published by SCHOCKEN BOOKS 1977

Second Printing, 1977

© 1970, 1972 by Ghetto Fighters' House and Hakibbutz Hameuchad Publishing House

Library of Congress Cataloging in Publication Data

Grossman, Mendel.
    With a camera in the ghetto.

    Translation of Tsalam hilekh ba-geto.
    Reprint of the ed. published by Ghetto Fighters'
    House, Lohame Hagetaot, Israel.
    1. Jews in Lódź; Poland—Pictorial works.
    2. Holocaust, Jewish (1939-1945)—Lódź, Poland—
    Pictorial works. 3. Lódź, Poland—History—Pictorial
    works. I. Kronika getta lódzkiego. II. Title.

DS135.P62L643513   1977   779′.9′9405315039240943 84   76-48815

Manufactured in the United States of America

THE DOCUMENTATION which took place during the Holocaust in the ghettos of Poland and Lithuania was a specific form of Jewish civil resistance. It was nurtured by a consciousness of history which the people developed when their very existence was in danger. The effort to leave testimony of all that transpired in the Jewish communities during the Nazi occupation became an expression of popular will. Young and old, even children, noted down events. Testimony was written by intellectuals who were accustomed to writing, and by simple folk who used the pen with difficulty. The written testimony was to constitute a bridge between the generation destined to perish and the one to arise after the Holocaust.

One member of this large family of chroniclers was Mendel Grossman, the photographer of the Lodz ghetto. What others wrote down with their pens he recorded with his camera. This album complements therefore already published material; and its visual-artistic aspect gives added significance to its documentary value.

The city of Lodz, which the Germans renamed Litzmannstadt, was the site of the first of the large ghettos in occupied Poland. The ghetto was established by an order published on February 8, 1940, and in May 1 of the same year it was finally closed off. Within its walls 160,000 Jews were imprisoned. Its area was 1.5 square miles; and it was located in the north of the city, a part which was the poorest in housing and sanitation. The political and security control of the ghetto was entrusted to the Gestapo, while police functions were carried out by the Kripo (Criminal Police). The German Gettoverwaltung (ghetto administration), which was subordinated to the German city mayor, was given the task of gradually depriving the Jewish population of all its property, of exploiting its labor potential, and eventually liquidating it. In the months of October–November, 1941, the ghetto population was increased by about 20,000 Jews, deportees from various German towns, as well as from Vienna, Prague, Luxemburg; and in the months May–August, 1942, by some tens of thousands of deportees from communities in the Lodz-Kalish area.

More than 43,000 persons died in the ghetto in the years 1940–44 from hunger and epidemics. This "slow" tempo of liquidation did not, however, fit in with the German plans for the "final solution."

Toward the end of 1941 a death camp was set up in Chelmno (Kulmhof), about 30 miles from Lodz, and in January, 1942, the first 10,000 Lodz Jews were taken there. The second wave of deportations, which affected 34,000 persons, came between February 22 and April 25 of the same year. After a short respite, 11,000 of the western Jews were sent to Chelmno, and in the days of September 5–12, 1942, came the most cruel of all deportations: 16,000 old people, children, and the sick were taken away. From then on the ghetto became a forced-labor camp.

In the middle of 1944, as the battlefront moved closer to Lodz, the final liquidation of the ghetto began: from June 23 until the beginning of September more than 60,000 Jews were sent to their deaths in Auschwitz-Birkenau. Only those meant to constitute a rear guard remained in the ghetto, and it was they who lived to be liberated on January 19, 1945, when the Red Army entered the city. Their number was 887.

In the Lodz ghetto there was no armed uprising, no insurrection of desperate people who have nothing to lose, of the kind which took place in many other Jewish communities of Poland under the Nazis. The main reason for this was the total isolation of the Lodz ghetto. The Germans succeeded in sealing it off more hermetically than any other ghetto in Poland. All attempts of the Jewish underground to breach the walls and penetrate it failed. The Polish underground in the area was weak and incapable of establishing contact with the people within the walls. Also, the Germans were successful in camouflaging their plans and in sowing confusion among the Jews. The Elder of the Jews, who "ruled" the ghetto by the authority of Germans, as well as the ramified staff he maintained, constituted an efficient instrument in the German hands for blunting the alertness of the ghetto inmates and implanting in them the illusion that obedience to orders and observance of strict work discipline would save the ghetto.

The photographs left by Mendel Grossman are a historical source of great importance for a deeper understanding of the suffering, the struggle for survival, and the eventual destruction of one Jewish community. They also transcend this task by helping to visualize the fate of ghetto prisoners everywhere. The devotion of this artist-photographer to his mission, his stubborn resistance to the surrounding reality, were not in vain.

CONTENTS

A view of the ghetto in the winter.

Friday, February 28, 1941

The weather:
Cloudy, 8°C. above 0.

Arrests:
14 were arrested today for theft, 15 for other
crimes, and one for resisting authority.

Deaths and births:
45 died today in the ghetto. No births were
registered.

Breadline in one of the ghetto streets.

Young and cheap manpower. Children pull a wagon. Children used to organize into groups in order to take on jobs, then divide the pay among themselves. *(preceding page)*

From the producer to the consumer. A young ghetto "farmer" sells his produce.

As customary in the ghetto, the soup is eaten where it is distributed.

"Litzmannstadt in the Future." This is the title of an article which appeared in the *Litzmannstadter Zeitung*. The article predicts that the part of town where the ghetto is now located will be covered by parks and lawns. After leveling the ground, magnificent buildings will be erected. The first stage of this plan is already being realized with the razing of houses on Ogrodowa and Nowomiejska streets, which adjoin the ghetto. As for the Jews now residing in the ghetto, the article states that "they will disappear sooner than they expect."

12

Human beasts of burden pull a wagon bringing supplies to the ghetto.

March 1, 1941

The population of the ghetto as of February 1, 1941, was 153,995; the number of inhabited rooms was 49,864, i.e., one room per 3 persons. . . . The number of deaths in February was 1,069, the number of births was 52. In comparison with January—the number of deaths then was 1,218—the decrease is considerable. It should be noted, incidentally, that the greatest mortality—1,366—caused by an epidemic of scarlet fever, was registered in July, 1940.

March 1, 1941

In the house on 42 Franciszkanska Street the body of a child in a state of total decay was discovered. The body was covered by rags.

A ghetto child.

The cemetery. In front is the gravestone of Israel Lichtenstein, a leader of the socialist
Bund party.

The Jewish cemetery of Lodz.

The doctor who was called to the place could not determine the exact day of the child's death, but stated that it happened at least two weeks ago. The child's father at first refused to give the reason why he did not bury the body of his only son, a boy of 7, but he later confessed that he did not bury the body in order to take advantage of the food coupons.

Deportees from towns in the area, arrive at the Lodz ghetto carrying their possessions.

A scene of the 1942 deportation. The deportees are Jews from Germany, Austria, Czechoslovakia, and Luxemburg who were brought to the ghetto in 1941.

Saturday, March 1, 1941

The Weather: Cloudy, about 6°C. above 0.

Arrests:
4 were arrested for theft, 3 for other crimes.

Death in the street: yesterday about 7 P.M. the
55-year-old Israel Wolf (15 Brzezinska Street)
collapsed on Koscielny Square. Despite quick
medical aid he died without regaining
consciousness.

A scene of the deportation. A woman writes her last letter before boarding the death train.

Jews from Germany, Czechoslovakia, Austria, and Luxemburg who were brought to the Lodz ghetto, are now being sent to the Chelmno death camp. Many of them were not strong enough to walk to the railroad station. The photograph shows the sick and the weak as they are being loaded onto a cart which will take them on their last journey. The year was 1942.

Scenes of the deportation, 1943.

Sunday, March 2, 1941

Yesterday, the inspector of the Housing Department discovered, while searching the flat of a certain Berek Gomberg, a hidden door leading to a room that did not figure in any register. The room was in a deplorable state. The shrewd Gomberg used the room as

Assembly place on Krawiecka Street for those condemned to deportation.

29

fuel; the floor, door, and window frames had
already been burned. Gomberg was arrested.
It is worth noting, incidentally, that the
destruction of housing for the purposes of fuel
has reached an improbable scale.

A church in the ghetto—a storehouse of ritual utensils
left after the deportation of the Jews.

The market on Bazarny Square. Here furniture was sold for fuel. Photographed in the winter of 1941.

Sunday March 2, 1941

The following amusing incident took place in one of the hospitals of the ghetto. A 5-year-old sick boy was brought there. When he was undressed, the attendants found a large piece of bread in a bag tied under his shirt. The boy categorically refused to part with the food.

Yom Kippur 1940. Services in the courtyard of an apartment house.

On the way to the deportation trains.

The Jews of Lodz enter the ghetto. Winter 1940.

33

Inside the church which served as storage house for bedding and feathers.

When he was told that he would receive full board in the hospital, he explained that the bread was his property, bought with his own money. How did he get it, the young patient was asked. "I have my own money because I am on relief," the determined child stated.

From March 10–24, 1941

At 8:30 P.M. on March 12 the 13-year-old Wolf Finkelsztajn of 14 Masarska Street was shot dead by the guards. He sustained fatal wounds in the lungs and heart. On March 19, about midnight, 31-year-old Rafal Krzepicki, born in Praszka and presently living on 12 Smugowa Street, was shot dead at the corner Franciszkanska and Smugowa. On March 23 at 9 P.M. 20-year-old Awigdor Lichtensztajn was shot dead at the septic ditches at the end of Franciszkanska Street, near the wire fence surrounding the ghetto.

Herszkowicz, a popular street singer who composed his own ballads based on current events.

A queue for food rations.

Tuesday March 25, 1941

Today was scheduled to take place the trial of Hersz Arager, who—as was noted in one of the previous bulletins—was guilty of the macabre act of concealing the body of his 7-year-old son in order to take advantage of the dead boy's food coupons. The man, however, died a day before the trial, and his wife Pesa was sent for a psychiatric examination.

July 22, 1941

It was recently discovered that flour furnished to the ghetto contains pieces of glass, stones, etc. It was recently discovered that the greens of young carrots and radishes can be eaten when they are cooked. The traffic in this product is now conducted on a large scale. . . .

Merchandise supplied to the ghetto is customarily of the lowest quality, faulty, spoiled, etc. . . . Wheat flour is of varied origin . . . the sacks are not full, the flour is often very hot, stale, hardened into lumps . . .

July 23, 1941

The Price Control Police found out that in some workshops potato pancakes were made of vegetable leftovers and potato peels . . .

Ghetto postman. The ghetto was hermetically closed off from the outside world but had an internal postal system.

Those working at transporting excrement were called in the ghetto argot "fecalists."

Searching for fuel in the ground.

They were called "coal miners" in the ghetto. They searched for fuel in the area where once factories discarded coal dust.

with an admixture of starch, and soda was added to flour. Candies were made of material that contains much sawdust ... a large percentage of ground brick was found in cocoa, cinnamon, pepper, etc... The easiest product to falsify is butter; unbelievable amounts of water—up to 70%—are kneaded into the fat, with potato starch added to make the mixture harder. ... The shaving soap "Samolin" is well suited for lining the inside of shoes because it contains pure talcum powder ...

A woman grubbing for fuel in the ground.

July 28, 1941

Deportation of the mentally ill.

About two months ago a German medical committee inspected the ghetto hospital for the mentally ill on Wesola Street. Yesterday two German doctors arrived at the hospital. At present 60 patients are hospitalized there. The management of the hospital showed the German doctors a list of 12 patients who were cured. Those were examined during the inspection, and five of them (two men and three women) were found fit to leave the hospital. The five were today sent home. As for the remaining patients, the hospital was given instructions to have them prepared for the next day to be sent out of the ghetto in two groups. Before they were taken away, the patients were given tranquilizing injections.

The deportation station on Czarniecki Street.

A woman waiting to be deported, pressing her face to the fence at the place of assembly on Czarniecki Street.

An old man in the ghetto. Photographed in 1940. Later, old people were no longer seen in the ghetto.

Leave-taking before deportation. Photographed in 1943.

Collecting dead bodies in the ghetto streets.

July 29, 1941

A woman was coming out of a distribution point carrying two breads when a starved looking man tore one of the loaves out of her hand and gobbled it up before anyone could stop him. He was beaten and taken to the office of the 3d District where a means was sought by which he could compensate for the robbery. The simplest way would have been that the man should give his victim two bread coupons so that the unfortunate woman should not have to starve. It turned out, however, that the robber had sold his coupons for a long period ahead. The question is, what to do?

A passage for vehicles and pedestrians at the corner of Dolna and Lotnicza streets. A German policeman guarded the passage. The road between the fences was not included in the ghetto.

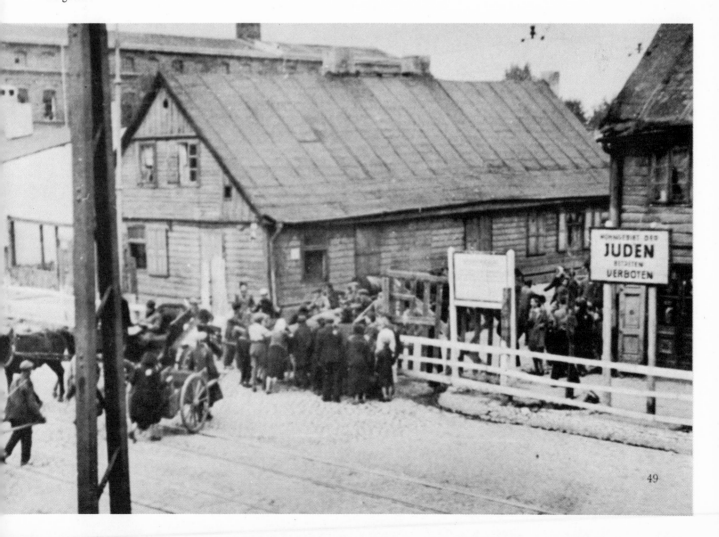

49

August 1, 1941

Though they are fully aware of the sad fate
that may await the sick, the families of those
needing hospitalization in mental homes make
every effort to have them admitted. The living
quarters are so crowded, the conditions so
squalid, that hospitalization means salvation
for the sick person's family. It is reported that
the first inmate was registered after the recent
purge.

The prices of vegetables reach improbable
heights; the outer leaves of cabbage (they
were used before to feed cattle; humans would
not eat them) cost 80 pfennigs; a head of
cabbage costs 2 marks.

The scarcity of fuel is such that in many
kitchens of private homes no fire has been lit
for months.

Corner Limanowska and Ciesielska streets where Jews passed to the other part of the ghetto.

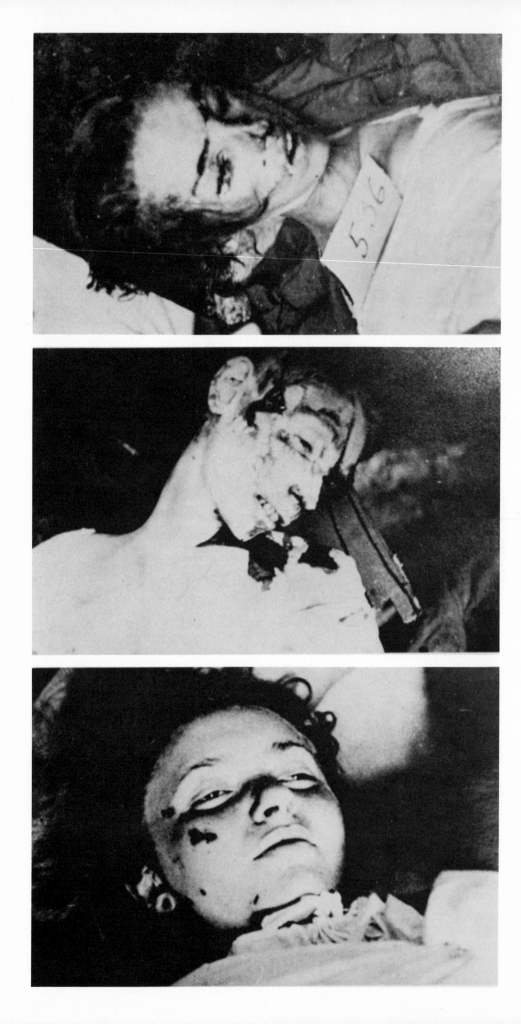

Victims of the great round-up in September, 1942.

One more grave in the cemetery.

Bread arrives at the distribution point.

August 4, 1941

A most characteristic trial recently took place
in the court. A dead, skinned horse was
brought to the garbage dump for burial, but
since it was already late in the day, the
burying was postponed till next morning. . . .

In the morning the attendants noticed that someone had cut off a piece of flesh from the horse's hind quarters. The guilty were found by the police and brought to court. They claimed that being in extreme need they had to do it in order to quiet their hunger. The sentence was 4 weeks.

September, 1941

Decrease in the bread ration.

Beginning with on September 20 the daily bread ration will be decreased from 400 to 300 grams. Thus a person now gets a loaf for 6 days instead of for 5 days as before.

Baking matzot in the ghetto. The year is 1940. In the following years matzot were no longer baked in the ghetto.

58

The elder brother.

A ghetto resident swallows his soup in the street.

September, 1941

A new transport of deportees arrived on the 29th of the month. The transport consisted of more than a thousand inhabitants of villages in the vicinity of Wloclawek. The deportees from villages in the Kujawy region wore different Jewish identification badges: in the middle of the back they had a yellow triangle, and hanging in front was a cut out Star of David, in size 25 cm.

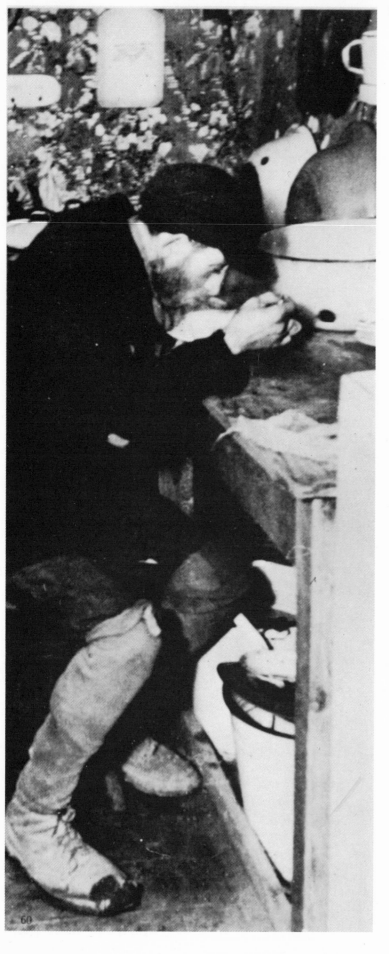

Bread is transported under guard from the bakery to a distribution point. The hungry gather around the wagons. *(overleaf)*

Transporting bread in the ghetto streets.

May 9–11, 1942

During the above three days 179 persons died in the ghetto . . .

One of the most sought after products is now potato peels. People find all sorts of ways to approach soup kitchen managers; all means of personal contacts are put in motion in order to get a bit of this food that for some is the only nutrition besides bread.

The saddest of all is the hunger . . . in the first half of April supply of all vegetables was stopped, and the population was reduced to rations consisting of 280 grams of bread and 250 grams of potatoes, the latter of the worst quality with many half-rotten pieces . . .

Women working at cleaning feathers eat their soup. The photograph was taken in the Church of the Holy Virgin. Here were stored featherbeds which remained after Jewish families of Lodz and vicinity were sent away.

The fence around the ghetto.

Lunch break for women working at cleaning feathers in the Church of the Holy Virgin. The feathers were taken from the bedding of Jewish families from Lodz and vicinity who perished in the Chelmno death camp.

A woman street cleaner. Photographed from the window of the photographer's apartment.

Wednesday, July 1, 1942

Today trucks brought to the courtyard of the Church of the Holy Virgin various packages of clothing, bedclothes, etc. Most packages were wrapped in tablecloths, bedsheets, and other linen. They were sorted out on the spot and stored away.

July 1, 1942

During the period from June 16 to July 1, 1942, the Re-employment Committee installed 1,600 more children in workshops. The number of children in workshops is now 11,000.

Children dig in the ground in search of fuel.

July 1, 1942

It is rumored that . . .
Yesterday, a persistent rumor was circulated in
the ghetto that any moment a notice would be
posted on the walls announcing an additional
food ration in the amount of 1.75 marks.
Unfortunately, the rumor proved false.

July 3, 1942

Received in the ghetto several days ago was a shipment of 800 kg. meat in a state of almost total decay.

July 18, 1942

There is a more than well-founded fear in the ghetto that in the near future an order will be given liquidating one or even more hospitals. The hospital buildings will be used for workshops.... Tuberculosis is the cause of 3–4 deaths each day, which decimates the population of the ghetto at a tempo much faster than during epidemics or at the fronts.

Deportees waiting to be sent away. Photographed on Krawiecka Street where the deportees were gathered before being loaded on trains.

July 21, 1942

Since the end of May, the ghetto has been receiving enormous quantities of clothing. Thus, until the 16th of this month the following articles arrived:

Clothing and rags	798,625 kg.
Feathers, feather beds, and pillows	221,035 ”
Furs and pelts	8,130 ”
Used footwear	69.50 ”
Used stockings and socks	50 ”
Used neckties	12 ”

July 21, 1942

Orders from the *Gettoverwaltung:*

The *Gettoverwaltung* ordered 250 sets of bedding and bedclothes for their own use to be made out of the recently received material. The order was carried out with the greatest accuracy, with the use of the best materials.

Women scavenging around a public kitchen, looking for scraps of food.

July 30, 1942

A loaf of bread is to last for 8 days. The news hit the population like a bolt from the blue. . . .

If no improvement comes soon, the situation may become fatal. Mortality—already reaching 70 deaths per day—may rise even more. . . .

One thing is certain: until now, the bread ration lasted for many ghetto inhabitants for 5 to 6 days, and they fasted on the remaining days. Now it will be even worse.

July 31, 1942

During the seven months of this year, more than 13,000 persons died, while only 11,500 died during the entire previous year. In 1940, before and after the ghetto period, the number of deceased was 8,200. The mortality of the recent months is frightening.

Children sell sweets in the streets. In the background, a winter landscape. Photographed in 1941.

Removing the snow and ice.

July 31, 1942

Burial difficulties:

There have been cases recently when bodies remained in the cemetery unburied for as long as 3–4 days. In the macabre lines in the pre-burial pavilions there are sometimes as many as 110 bodies. The Burial Department has at its disposal 4 horses, of which one is sick.

August 1, 1942

Liquidation of the last vestiges of teaching:

Day before yesterday the chairman ordered a stop until further notice of all classes, talks, and lectures that were still taking place in the

Jews copying the details of the announcement concerning new food rations.

Ghetto streets in the winter.

youth clubs in Marysin. Thus, all education in the ghetto has been liquidated. The original order came from outside.... It is reported from other sources ... that the bread rations will be given only once in 10 days.

August 6, 1942

New kind of hearse:

A new kind of hearse has been plying the ghetto for several days now. It is a huge platform pulled by one horse. On the platform is a box of rough planks that opens at the top. This peculiar hearse can take as many as 30 dead bodies at one time ...

August 24, 1942

The increasing number of cases of typhus has made it necessary to post an announcement with the commonly known instructions on keeping clean and careful ...

August 25, 1942

For the past two weeks the air has been unusually dry with a temperature reaching 40°C. This has done great harm to cabbage, which has been eaten up in the entire ghetto by insects. Where only yesterday was a beautiful head of cabbage, one can now see only skeletons of leaves.

The once beautiful cabbage patches, the true pride of those who worked hard and with devotion, now stand abandoned and empty ... the masses of insects have given them a different color, that is how thickly they cover them. No one remembers a plague of such dimensions ... it developed faster than it

could be coped with. . . . A large number of
leaves simply rotted, and thus rotted and
vanished the fruit of the labor of so many
hands, so much blood and last bits of strength.
What this means can be understood only by
those who fell victim to the plague, the people
who worked alone or with their families. Now
the little man stands lost, embarrassed. He had
thought that his labor of Sisyphus could
provide something for the coming difficult
winter, he had believed in a better tomorrow
. . . and now suddenly there is nothing but
disappointment and despair.

August 28, 1942

Jews from Pabianic, Belchatow, Ozorkow,
Zelow, Wielun, Strykow, Sieradz, Lask, and
recently also from Zdunska Wola have
arrived, and the transports have not yet
stopped. At the same time, bedding is being
brought from those towns, no longer on trucks
but on wagonettes running on tramcar lines.
This new development occupies all minds. The
arrivals tell stories of what they have gone
through recently, and all stories are permeated
with pain and despair. They arrived, were
assigned to different places, and it is difficult
to understand why some got to the ghetto
while others had to travel an even sadder
road. . . . Again the ghetto is full of a strange
uncertainty; the people are tormented by

Peddlers of homemade sweets and saccharine.

A queue in front of the Jewish post office.

Posted lists of places where services were to take place on the High Holidays.
The year is 1940. From then on public services were forbidden.

Mordechai Chaim Rumkowski, the German-appointed Elder of the Jews (Aelteste der Juden).

Distribution of relief money on behalf of the community. The year is 1940.

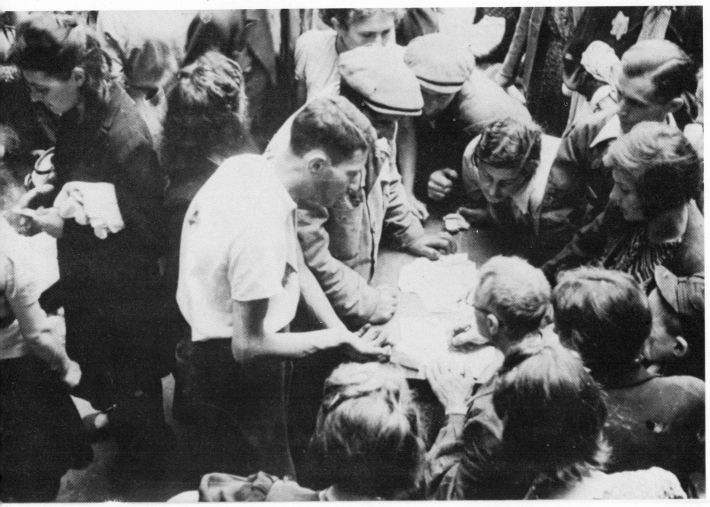

The ruins of the synagogue on Wolborska Street after the fire and explosion. The synagogue was set on fire in 1939 and blown up in 1940.

stories told by the arrivals, and the great unknown is worse than the worst reality. . . . It is known that the food stores are empty. . . . The most important, most vital question is how to live on the food ration; for about 95% of the population it is a matter of life, of survival . . . still this matter has now been pushed into the background, and only in whispers does one talk about rations. More

important are the experiences of brothers from villages, their pain and suffering. One can see in the ghetto pale shadows of human beings with swelling on their hands and faces, deformed bodies, whose only dream is to last and survive . . . survive until a better tomorrow without new difficulties, at the cost, perhaps, of a smaller and worse food ration.

The vicinity of the synagogue on Wolborska Street after the explosion. The wall belonged to the house of study.

September 1, 1942

Before the curfew a truck with two trailers
drew up to the hospital on Wesola Street, and
the representatives of the authorities who
accompanied the vehicle . . . demanded that
all patients be taken out. From Wesola Street
the truck went to the hospital on Drewnowska
Street and took the patients. . . . The same
happened in the hospital at the Lagiewnicka
and Mickiewicza Streets.

At the first hospital all patients were
evacuated, at the second—it is told—some
saved themselves by escaping, while at the
latter two the patients are said to have jumped
over the hospital fence. . . .

Here a brother, here a sister, here a father,
a mother, a cousin, an aunt. Each of them lost
someone. Such despair was never seen in the
ghetto, even during the deportations. Never
was so much lamenting heard. Here and there
stood groups of weeping women, children, and
helpless men who parted from their loved
ones in such a tragic manner.

Families working at loading and carrying excrement pass the streets of the ghetto. *(overleaf)*

Emptying the excrement containers into ditches on Franciszkanska Street.

September 1, 1942

Meantime life goes on, wagons with potatoes arrive and make up for other troubles. He who was not personally hurt thinks of tomorrow and believes that fate will save him from another terrible trial. Minds are blunted, and the important matter is now to fill one's belly.

September 14, 1942

One week, 8 days, which seem to have been an eternity.

It is still difficult to realize what took place. A hurricane passed through the ghetto taking along 15,000 persons (no one knows the exact number), and life seems to have returned to the old rut.

September 14, 1942

A representative of the Gestapo entered every home.... A pistol was the signal for all inhabitants of a building to come down to the courtyard where they were arranged in double rows, and the representatives of the authorities inspected them. Meantime the police searched the homes and brought down those who were hiding and the sick.

Those to be deported were placed on one side of the courtyard, and those to remain on the other.

The artist Leizerowicz against the background of the bridge on Koscielny Square.

The view under the bridge. Change of guard. The ghetto was guarded
by German gendarmes.

September 14, 1942

What will happen next no one knows. Some
order must be established because many
families use the food coupons of the deported
relatives and neighbors, while in other families
the deported took along the cards of the whole
family. Monstrous stories are being told: one
concerns a woman who was deported with her
three children, took all coupons, and left her
husband to die after he had not eaten in five
days. Some were taken away while they were
queuring up to receive potatoes and dairy
products and with them were taken the food
coupons of entire families that remained with
nothing.

The bridge over Zgierska Street connecting the two parts of the ghetto.
The road below was not included in the ghetto.

Excrement carriers in the ghetto streets. In the background is a breadline. It was customary that whole families, father, mother, and children, did this work. Despite the fact that they received extra food rations, they did not stay alive long. The task was eventually given as a punishment for breaking ghetto ordinances, when there were no more volunteers for the job.

September 21, 1942

In the building on 34/36 Lagiewnicka Street, which once housed the Health Department and Hospital No. 1, a carpentry workshop will now be established.

October 22, 1942

The bridge on Koscielna Square again became the scene of a suicide. Frajda-Ruchla Dobrzynska, age 45, born in Lodz on 38 Zgierska Street, jumped off the upper level of the bridge to the street below at 5:45 P.M. She sustained heavy injuries. Her husband, Icek Dobrzynski, age 46, committed suicide yesterday by jumping from a fourth-floor window. Frajda-Ruchla initially tried to follow her husband by coming near the ghetto fence, but the guard did not use his rifle. When this failed, she jumped from the bridge. The cause of both suicides are the deportations, several weeks earlier. Their two children were taken away.

November 20, 1942

Various rumors were circulated yesterday in the ghetto concerning the potato ration; there was talk about 4 kg. and about 5 kg. In the evening it became clear that there was going to be no potato ration at all.

November 21, 1942

A concert.

Tonight a concert took place in the House of
Culture under the direction of Bajgelman. The
program consisted of light operetta music. The
Viennese singer Bandler appeared,
accompanied by a piano.

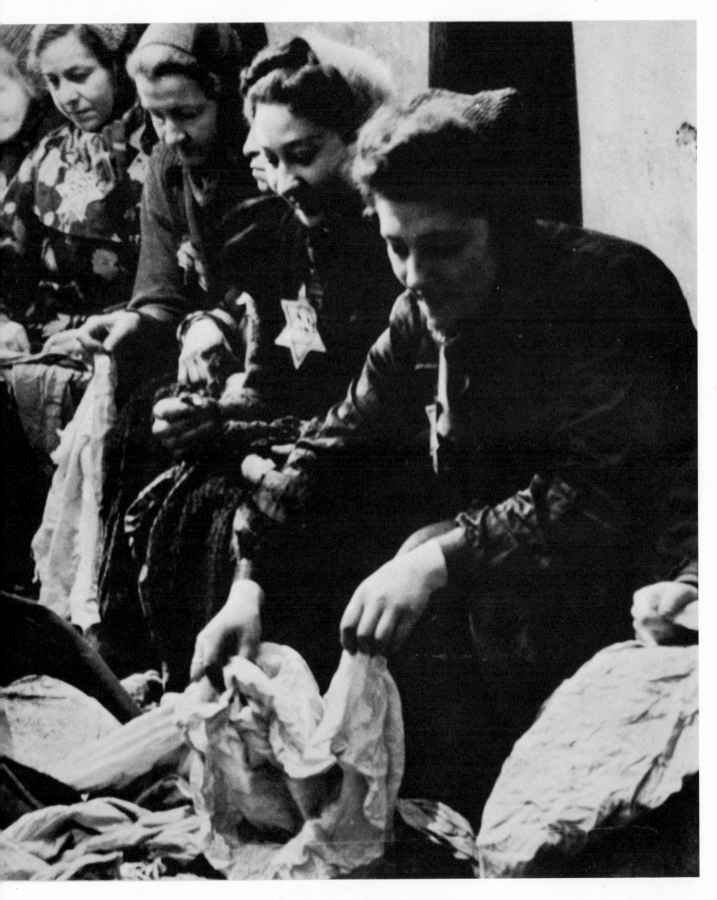

Women sort out objects brought to the ghetto after Jewish communities in the vicinity of
Lodz were liquidated.

Thursday, December 3, 1942

The weather:

Cold, snow, temperature below 0.
Deaths:

27 persons. One child was born (dead). . . . In
the central jail the execution took place of
three young girls who were condemned to
death by a firing squad for escaping from a
labor camp in Poznan. The executed are:
Matla Rozensztajn, born December 15, 1921,
in Radom; Sure Jamniak, born May 2, 1914,
in Lodz; and Gitl Hadasa Aronowicz, born
June 22, 1925. . . .

The inhabitants of the ghetto were greatly
cheered by the news that the highest
authorities in Berlin recognized the ghetto as a
labor camp.

A view of the ghetto in the winter.

MENDEL GROSSMAN—THE PHOTOGRAPHER OF THE LODZ GHETTO

by Arieh Ben-Menahem

Drawings and photographs by Mendel Grossman

HE WAS A SLIM MAN of less than average height, with sloping shoulders, his coat hanging on him as if it was not cut to his size, even his shoes appearing too large for him. His eyes expressed goodness, a clever smile played on his lips. His steps were measured, and he always carried a stuffed briefcase. That was Mendel Grossman, a young man of a hasidic family, the type of a former talmudic student who had left the straight and narrow path. He was avid for knowledge, a lover of literature, the theater and the arts, a painter, a sculptor, and also an amateur photographer who believed that photography was an art, and that the development of abstract painting did not detract from the camera as a tool in the hands of a creator but, on the contrary, opened up new horizons to be exploited. His painter friends disagreed with him, and Mendel made every effort to prove the truth of his argument. His photographs—

flowers, still lifes, landscapes, street scenes, portraits taken against the background of clouds—were works of art filled with expression, leaving strong impressions on the viewer. At the same time he did not give up painting. The subject of his paintings were the same as of his photographs: still lifes, the human figure, groups, the street. The paintings and photographs had a clear bond. When one compared the two, it became quite obvious that they were the works of the same artist.

Eventually Mendel Grossman began to concentrate on one subject—man in motion. The transition came abruptly, and by accident. The Habimah theater was visiting Lodz, and Mendel, hidden in the wings, photographed the performances. No one asked him to do it; he did it for himself alone. Here were men and women in motion, in classical motion: there was dancing, varied and strange facial expres-

sions, laughter, fear, pain, as well as make up, costumes, light, stage settings. When later he locked himself in his darkroom to develop the films, he was astonished by the power of his photographs; he actually succeeded in arresting men in motion. All those who saw the pictures extolled their excellence, but Mendel knew that he was only at the beginning of the road. Habimah left, and Mendel directed his lens to the street, to the suburbs inhabited by Jews, the slums. He now found motion and expression not on the stage, but in the streets, among children playing, laborers at work in the Jewish quarter of Baluty. Here, too, he achieved impressive results. In the fiery discussions with artist friends on the meaning of the plastic arts he convinced not with words but with the results of his camera work.

His photographs gained a measure of respect, and Mendel achieved recognition as an artist-photographer. In the beginning of 1939, the management of TOZ, the Jewish organization for the protection of child health, approached him with an attractive proposition—to prepare an album of pictures of Jewish children. The accent was to be on the poor Jewish child in the streets. Mendel accepted the proposition enthusiastically, and was soon ready with a series of photographs. It was summer 1939. The album never appeared. The photographs got lost in the war, and at the same time perished their subject— the Jewish child.

The idyllic life of discussions on the meaning of the plastic arts ceased with the outbreak of the war. There came the great upheavals, the panic, the escapes, the first confrontation with the brutal occupier, then the yellow patch to denote the Jew, and the ghetto, the first days of becoming adjusted to a new reality, of finding new living quarters. Mendel was ready with his camera. No longer did he photograph flowers, clouds, still lifes, landscapes. In the surrounding horror he had found his mission: to photograph and thus to record the great tragedy taking place in the ghetto before his eyes.

Again there was man in motion, but that was a unique kind of motion—motion toward death. His eyes again saw fear and anger, faces full of expression. But this time it was hunger not makeup that changed the facial features, poverty that created the costumes, disintegrating hovels that served as stage sets, with barbed wire in the background.

Mendel Grossman knew how to photograph. He knew how to observe and perceive what happened around him, and what is most important—he saw the people surrounding him. He photographed them in their suffering, as they sank into the depths of pain, in their struggles, in their illnesses, and in their death. He recorded with his camera what took place in the tortured ghetto, the Holocaust at its intensity.

He gave up his artistic ambitions of the past. His mission was now clear: to leave to the world—if a world was to remain—a tangible testimony of the great tragedy, of the horrible crime, in a language understood by all nations.

Evicted from his house in the center of town, Mendel found a flat in the ghetto where he settled with his parents, two sisters, brother-in-law, and little nephew.

The story of his family is typical of Jewish families in Lodz. Mendel realized this, and intensively photographed his loved ones, so that over the years he created a horrifying record of their slow progress toward death.

Mendel wangled a job in the photographic laboratory of the department of statistics in the ghetto, the office in which all the true information concerning the ghetto was collected. Covered by its official status, the staff of the department accumulated written material. They did not only record dry facts, as statisticians usually do, but wrote down every rumor passing through the ghetto, every change in the distribution of food rations, every event no matter how unimportant. They also collected photographs, ostensibly to demonstrate models of products of the ghetto workshops, and identification photographs for work permits. The laboratory had a good supply of film and printing paper, and also served as an ideal camouflage for Mendel's real job. He spent most of the time in the streets, in the narrow alleys, in homes, in soup kitchens, in bread lines, in workshops, at the cemetery. The chief subject was people.

He did not seek beauty, for there was no beauty in the ghetto. There were children bloated with hunger, eyes searching for a crust of bread, living "death notices," as those near death but still on their feet were called in ghetto slang, convoys of men and women condemned to death in the ovens of Chelmno, public executions. There were men pulling wagons, there was pain, agonies, and death. The people knew Mendel and wanted him to photograph them. In one incident, a whole family passed through the street dragging a wagon filled with excrement, a father, mother, son, and daughter, the parents in front pulling, and the children pushing from the sides. Mendel stopped but did not take out his camera; he hesitated to photograph the degradation of those people. But the head of the family halted and asked Mendel to photograph. "Let it remain for the future, let others know how humiliated we were." Mendel no longer hesitated. He gave in to that urge which motivated so many of the best of our people: to leave a record, to write down the events, to collect documents, to scratch a name on the wall of the prison cell, to write next to the name of the condemned the word "vengeance."

Mendel had heart trouble, and he was forbidden to make any physical effort. The Gestapo was also on his tracks, and his friends warned him, his family insisted that he stop endangering his life. But he did not heed any warnings. No event in the ghetto passed without him photographing it. To fool the police he carried his camera under his coat. He kept his hands in his pockets, which were cut open inside, and he thus could manipulate the camera. He directed the lens by turning his body in the direction he wanted, then slightly parted his coat, and clicked the shutter. This method worked very well.

In one of the stages of the destruction of the Jewish people, the Germans deported the remnants of the Jewish communities of Germany, Austria, Czechoslovakia, and Luxemburg, and brought them to the Lodz ghetto. The deportees were not told where they were going. The Germans fed them stories about a "Jewish autonomous region." Mendel received the arrivals with camera in hand. Here were characters of a new kind, with a different appearance, different manners. They were well dressed, they carried heavy suitcases, were well provided with food. They were horror stricken at the sight of the ghetto, refused to become members of it. They spoke of culture, of hygiene, made attempts at living in a manner they had been accustomed to. They refused contact with the old inhabitants of the ghetto whose appearance repelled them. They tried to swim against the current and quickly gave up. Their capitulation was cruel. They fell prey to diseases of the ghetto, to the dirt, the lice; they collapsed spiritually and physically. Mendel and his camera followed this process, and thus we had a record of this tragic development which ended when the Germans collected the pitiful remnants and again loaded them on trains. This time the trains were bound for Chelmno.

One of them, a Jew from Vienna in his late fifties, made an attempt to escape from the ghetto and succeeded in getting through the barbed wire. He had reached the railroad station, but there, when he took out his handkerchief, the yellow patch he had taken off his clothes fell out of his pocket, a Gestapo man noticed it, and he was arrested. Soon the ghetto inhabitants were ordered to congregate in the Bazarny Square to witness his execution.

Mendel decided to photograph the event, hidden in a room with a window overlooking the square. The photograph taken at a long distance was not satisfactory, the details were not clear enough. But everyone knew that the Germans would furnish more opportunities to photograph executions. And soon, on a cloudy day, he again ventured out with his camera, this time to an open field, on Marysinska Street. Unlike the first time, Mendel did not take up a protected position, but stood right there, behind a German policeman, in the front row of the crowd. As usual, the camera was suspended from a strap around his neck, the coat was slightly parted, and his hands under the coat directed the lens to the scaffold.

The condemned, a young man, was brought in a cart. He still did not realize what was going to happen to him. He noticed at first a large crowd, and then the dangling noose. Now he knew. Without uttering a sound he ascended the scaffold, his head down. The crowd held its breath. The distant cries of the condemned man's wife also ceased. The Germans were tense as the hangman tightened the noose around the victim's neck. Mendel clicked the shutter. The silence was so absolute that even this muted sound reached the ears of a German policeman, and he turned his head.

Pale with excitement, Mendel returned to the small darkroom in his flat to develop the picture. This time the photograph was clear in every detail. Still Mendel thought that he should change his technique. From then on he climbed electric power posts to photograph a convoy of deportees on their way to the trains, he walked roofs, climbed the steeple of a church that remained within the confines of the ghetto in order to photograph a change of guard at the barbed-wire fence. Weak and sick, he found it difficult to accomplish all those feats, but he was contemptuous of danger and did not heed pleadings of friends. Inside the church he discovered a strange world—a surrealistic picture which could be only the product of morbid fantasy: the entire interior was covered with a thick layer of white feathers. Waves of feathers rose into the air with each step, each movement. Every breeze caused a cloud of feathers to form in the air. The altar of carved wood, the figures of the saints, and the huge organ—all were covered with feathers, all undulated in the breeze. Amidst all that he saw human figures, also wrapped in white, sitting, running around, standing. The picture was strange and frightening, and the darkness of the Gothic interior added to the weirdness of the scene. A small sign attached to the entrance attempted to explain what was happening inside. It read Institute for Feather Cleaning. But the sign did not tell the whole truth. That was the place to which the bedding robbed from Jews who were sent to death from Lodz and surrounding towns was being brought. There, in the Church of the Virgin Mary, the pillows and featherbeds were ripped open by Jewish men and women, then the feathers were cleaned, sorted, packed, and shipped to Germany, to merchants who sold them in the Reich. It was hard work, and there seemed to be no end to it. Mendel spent many weeks in the church. Covered with feathers, he looked for varied angles which would fully explain to future generations what was happening in that church. He created evidence of the crime, the full extent of which was not yet known to him. Only his intuition told him that this must be recorded.

An order of the authorities called for the evacuation of an entire block of houses in the ghetto. Various rumors immediately spread, and the full meaning of the order soon became clear: carloads of German-speaking Gypsies were arriving. The Germans settled them in the evacuated houses and separated them from the Jewish inhabitants of the ghetto by a well-guarded barbed-wire fence. Soon an air of horror began to emanate from that camp; screams of children and adults accompanied by the sound of music were being heard there day and night. Criminal Police men settled with the Gypsies, a fact boding no good for them, but soon the Germans started running away when an epidemic of typhus broke out there. This meant that the camp was to be liquidated. The carts that once a day used to carry the dead to the ghetto cemetery began to travel back and forth several times during the day to keep up with the supply of dead bodies. In the ghetto new rumors spread concerning the real identity of the Gypsies.

Mendel was, as usual, on the job, looking for an opportunity to record the developments within the ghetto, but he did not succeed very well. The photographs taken from windows and roofs of houses facing the Gypsy ghetto were not clear. When finally the order came for the Gypsies to leave, and they were chased out in a bedlam of shouts and rifle fire on their way to the Chelmno crematorium, Mendel entered the abandoned houses in search of clues that would help identify the victims. He acquired a special kind of film which was sensitive to infrared rays, and with it he photographed every mark, every inscription, no matter how illegible, on the walls and doors, and he managed to decipher some of the names of the persons who lived there.

The collection of negatives grew from day to day, its contents became richer and more varied. The negatives were hidden in round tin cans, among them a can full of negatives from the performances of Habimah in Lodz in 1938. Mendel again and again stressed in conversations with friends that he expected those negatives eventually to reach Tel Aviv and be given to the theater. He did not speak of plans for the future, he only wanted his photographs to be exhibited as testimony of what took place in the ghetto.

Again he went out into the streets to photograph. He always found a subject. Sometimes acquaintances gave him clues.

The desire to record, to record at all cost, had become part of the consciousness of the inhabitants of the ghetto. All parts of the community had become permeated by this desire, and Mendel with his camera was received with open arms and with full understanding in workshops, in hospitals, in orphanages, in offices, in the streets. People exposed to him their troubles, showed their wounds, opened the doors of their homes. Let him come in and photograph, let it become known to all those who did not know, to those who would otherwise not believe.

The year was 1942. The Germans announced a new deportation from the ghetto, a deportation on a scale much vaster and performed in a manner much more cruel than the previous ones. A strict curfew was clamped down, and in five days Gestapo, Kripo (Criminal Police), and policemen went from home to home selecting Jews for death. There were those who tried to evade them, only to fall under German bullets. The dead bodies were collected and thrown in a heap on the cemetery, where there was no one to bury them. In the meantime, those selected for death were held in the hospitals, which at that time were already empty because the sick had been the first to be sent to Chelmno.

Mendel decided that here was a subject he must not miss. The danger was great because it was forbidden to be in the streets, but this did not stop him. The bodies were beginning to decompose in the heat, and fearing an epidemic, the Germans ordered them immediately buried. A number of gravediggers and laborers were given permission to leave their houses and proceed to the cemetery. Mendel attached himself to them, with camera in hand. Carts continued to bring bodies, but Mendel first turned his attention to the open mass grave. Inside were deportees from the nearby town Zdunska Wola. They had died of suffocation in the tightly packed trains. Mendel managed to take the pictures before the gravediggers did their job of covering the evidence. Then, with his slow step he went to the hall reserved for memorials but which was now filled with bodies. From the distance the sound of rifle fire was heard; the action continued. While photographing, Mendel marked the chests with numbers. The same numbers later appeared on the graves, and thus the families were able to identify the graves by first identifying their dead on the photographs. The head of each body was lifted by a gravedigger, and Mendel went from one to another clicking, recording the bruised, bloody, crushed faces, faces of old people, of boys, and of girls. Some of the eyes were closed, some half open, some stared with fear, some exuded the serenity of death.

It was autumn and still hot, and the stench was causing dizziness and nausea. A black hearse kept bringing fresh transports of bodies, and Mendel, tired and perspiring, stayed on the job. He bent over each face after photographing and wiped off the soot left by the exploding magnesium, and chased away the flies. He was pale and breathed with difficulty. The others told him that this was no job for a man with a bad heart, but he paid no attention, and did not even consent to rest a while. He must record this crime, otherwise no one would believe it. He went out for a while to breathe some fresh air, wiped off the perspiration, rinsed his face with cold water, and returned to the dark, stinking hall to continue his work, with the same zeal, with the same stubbornness. He tried to protect himself from the stench by tying a handkerchief around his mouth and nose, but soon took it off, for it interfered with the work. Clouds of flies swarmed in the air. Mendel gave up wiping them off his face, he only kept them off the lens.

The great deportation action was about to end. The Germans finished the chase and the murder in the ghetto. Mendel still managed to photograph the large wagons full of Jews condemned to death as they made their way to the concentration places and from there to the railroad station. Again the trains rolled in the direction of Chelmno, and the installations of "Sonderkommando-Bottman" worked at full speed.

There followed "regular" days in the ghetto, and one could find Mendel in the streets and ghetto institutions, his lens directed toward the starving and the sick who were not allowed to be sick because there was no room for them in the ghetto, and therefore all medical institutions were liquidated. They remained only in Mendel's photographs.

In 1943 deportations again began. The inhabitants of the ghetto still did not know to where the deportees were being taken; there were many rumors, most of them pessimistic, but some contained grains of hope. Mendel sensed that the omens were bad; he suspected the Germans of taking the deportees to a place from which there was no return.

He photographed almost exclusively the convoys, the places where the deportees were concentrated, the ghetto jail. Friends warned him against photographing the convoys, because Gestapo men were among the guards, and they would find him out. Again he heeded no warnings. In one of the ghetto workshops, a telescopic lens was being secretly constructed for him according to a sketch he prepared. When completed, the lens performed satisfactorily, but was heavy and awkward to carry. Mendel was happy, because he could now photograph from a distance and from hiding. He photographed the convoys from windows, following them until the deportees entered the death trains. He was in great danger when photographing the railroad station with the German police pushing the Jews into the trains. He took the photographs hidden behind a stack of slabs of concrete belonging to a factory of prefabricated houses. The new lens did its work well.

Mendel showed particular interest in recording the activites of youth organizations in the ghetto. He appeared at meetings, photographed events. All was open to him. The young people trusted him, and Mendel discovered suddenly smiling faces, faith in the future, and care for fellow men. When he was asked with which of the youth movements he identified himself, he evaded answering with his characteristic smile. There were no longer orphanages and old people's homes in the ghetto, and so he photographed the children in the workshops to which the entire population was mobilzed.

A new subject: children at work, old people at work. And from this subject he turned to another and greatly different one. He infiltrated the parties of the ghetto potentates and their coteries, photographed their shameful mode of living, which was a mockery of the sufferings of the starving population. Many of Mendel's pictures showed the institutions of the ghetto authorities. They stressed the bitter irony of the "autonomy" given to the Jews

within the barbed-wire fence, the empty paraphernalia: offices, police, parades, uniforms.

He generously distributed copies of his photographs. He asked for no payment; he let the pictures be kept by as many people as possible. Perhaps some would remain after the Holocaust. There were many takers, especially his artist friends. He had many friends; he did not suffer from loneliness. Many offered him help, many aided him in his daily problems of living. There were those who counted it a privilege to accompany him in the ghetto streets and carry his heavy satchel. And there were those who wanted to forget for a while their own troubles sitting with him in the darkroom and watching an image slowly emerge on the film as he held it in the liquid—another item in the large collection of the photographed history of the destruction of a people.

When Mendel's friends needed help, they knew that he would never refuse to do whatever possible. He would not forget to take along a friend when he went to photograph in a place where he expected that soup or potatoes would be served, and he would share it with his companion.

He spent his evenings locked in his darkroom, working till late at night. In the mornings he distributed prints among friends and acquaintances and kept only the negatives for himself. He dismissed every thought of the danger to which he was

exposed. He kept next to his enlarging apparatus a little crystal set with an earphone which was capable of receiving only the German radio station in Lodz. Thus he was informed on the progress of the war, but he did not indulge in commenting on the subject. He had a big job to do, and he continued to stalk the streets of the ghetto, recording on film the agony of the Jewish community of Lodz. His drawers were full of tin cans with more than ten thousand negatives, the result of hard and stubborn work of four and one half years. Those cans contained the images of people whose ashes were already scattered in the forests of Chelmno. In them was the story of the suffering and destruction of a great Jewish community, the most telling proof of the greatest crime in human history.

In the second half of 1944, the defeat of the Nazis seemed certain and close. When the remaining inhabitants of the ghetto heard the thunder of cannon on the approaching front, an order came for the final liquidation of the ghetto.

Mendel knew that he must now hide his treasure in a safe place. It must eventually reach the hands of those who would survive until liberation, and if no one would, then those who have not known the Holocaust should have them. Mendel made a quick selection of negatives, packed the tin cans in a wooden crate. With the help of a friend he took out a window sill in his apartment, removed some bricks, placed the crate in the hollow, then replaced the sill. The task was accomplished. The treasure seemed safe for the future. But still Mendel did not give up his camera.

The days of the liquidation came. There was chaos everywhere. Mendel continued to photograph to the very end. He could no longer develop the film. The ghetto was almost empty; only here and there someone would pass at a run. Trains left twice a day for an unknown destination. One of the last to leave was Mendel, the camera hidden under his coat. Several days later the Gestapo got wind of his activities when they found in some abandoned flats prints of his photographs—the definite proof of their own crime. They looked for him in ghetto, but he was no longer there. Alone, separated from his family and friends, Mendel arrived at a work camp in Germany. He still had his camera and used it as long as he had some strength left. Several days before the German surrender the Nazis evacuated the camp, and the inmates were again on the road.

Mendel's weak heart could no longer stand this effort. He collapsed on the road, the camera still with him. He was 32 at his death.

When the war ended, the negatives were taken out of their hiding place by Mendel's sister and were sent to Israel. Ten thousand negatives reached Kibbutz Nitzanim in the south. When the kibbutz fell into Egyptian hands during the War of Independence, the treasure was lost. Only few of the many hundreds of prints, those that Mendel distributed among his friends and acquaintances, remained.

One of Mendel's closest friends, Nahman Sonnabend, remained in the ghetto until liberation. Although the Nazis kept him under constant surveillance, he succeeded in saving the archives of the Judenrat, and he concealed the documentary treasure, including some of Mendel's photographs, at the bottom of a well. After the war the material was taken out of Poland.

They were collected, and are now exhibited at the Museum of Holocaust and Resistance at the Ghetto Fighters' House in Kibbutz Lohame Hagetaot, Israel.